My Store Scavenger Hunt

Bela Davis

Abdo Kids Junior
is an Imprint of Abdo Kids
abdobooks.com

Abdo
SENSES SCAVENGER HUNT
Kids

abdobooks.com

Published by Abdo Kids, a division of ABDO, P.O. Box 398166, Minneapolis, Minnesota 55439.
Copyright © 2023 by Abdo Consulting Group, Inc. International copyrights reserved in all countries.
No part of this book may be reproduced in any form without written permission from the publisher.
Abdo Kids Junior™ is a trademark and logo of Abdo Kids.

Printed in the United States of America, North Mankato, Minnesota.

052022

092022

THIS BOOK CONTAINS
RECYCLED MATERIALS

Photo Credits: Getty Images, Shutterstock

Production Contributors: Teddy Borth, Jennie Forsberg, Grace Hansen

Design Contributors: Candice Keimig, Pakou Moua

Library of Congress Control Number: 2021950708

Publisher's Cataloging-in-Publication Data

Names: Davis, Bela, author.

Title: My store scavenger hunt / by Bela Davis.

Description: Minneapolis, Minnesota : Abdo Kids, 2023 | Series: Senses scavenger hunt | Includes online
    resources and index.

Identifiers: ISBN 9781098261573 (lib. bdg.) | ISBN 9781644948385 (pbk.) | ISBN 9781098262419
    (ebook) | ISBN 9781098262839 (Read-to-Me ebook)

Subjects: LCSH: Senses and sensation--Juvenile literature. | Grocery stores--Juvenile literature. | Scavenger
    hunting--Juvenile literature.

Classification: DDC 612.8--dc23

Table of Contents

Store Scavenger Hunt

Let's go on a hunt! Can we find these things at a store?

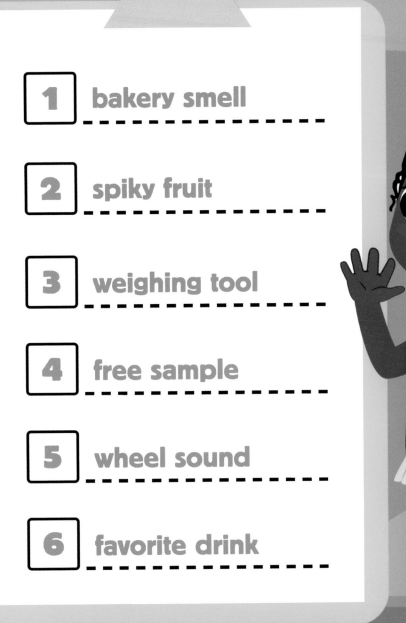

1 **bakery smell** -

2 **spiky fruit** -

3 **weighing tool** - - - - - - - - - - - - - - - - - - -

4 **free sample** -

5 **wheel sound** -

6 **favorite drink** - - - - - - - - - - - - - - - - - -

We have five **senses**. They can help find things.

I smell with my nose.

I smell a muffin.

I feel with my hand. I feel
a **spiky** pineapple.

I see with my eye.

I see a scale.

ORGANIC ORGANIC ORGANIC ORGANIC

Valencia ORANGES
¢1.49 lb

PINK GRAPEFRUIT
¢2.49 ea.

Anjou PEARS
¢2.89 ¢

LIMES
59¢

TOMATOES
¢2.49 lb

LEMONS
¢1.19

AVOCADOS
¢1.89

GARLIC
¢8.59

¢1.69

¢2.39

¢2.49

¢1.39

¢1.39

DAIRY

13

I taste with my tongue.

I taste yummy cheese.

I hear with my ear.

I hear a noisy cart.

I see with my eye.

I see milk.

19

We found all 6 things!
Can you find them in your store? Happy hunting!

Make Your Own Scavenger Hunt

Decide Where to Go

Make a List of Things
You May Find

Add Senses to That List

Find Your Things!

Glossary

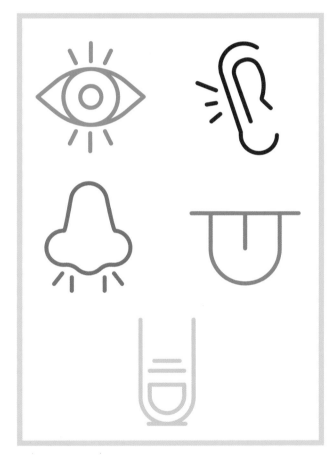

sense
any of five ways to experience one's surroundings. The senses are sight, hearing, smell, taste, and touch.

spiky
long and sharp-pointed.

Index

Abdo Kids ONLINE
FREE! ONLINE MULTIMEDIA RESOURCES

Visit **abdokids.com** to access crafts, games, videos, and more!

Use Abdo Kids code
SMK1573
or scan this QR code!

24